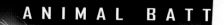

GIANT OTTER VS. CAIMAN

BY KIERAN DOWNS

Torque brims with excitement
perfect for thrill-seekers of all kinds.
Discover daring survival skills, explore
uncharted worlds, and marvel at mighty
engines and extreme sports. In *Torque* books,
anything can happen. Are you ready?

This edition first published in 2022 by Bellwether Media, Inc.

Library of Congress Cataloging-in-Publication Data

Names: Downs, Kieran, author.
Title: Giant otter vs. caiman / by Kieran Downs.
Other titles: Giant otter versus caiman
Description: Minneapolis, MN : Bellwether Media, Inc., 2022. | Series:
  Torque: animal battles | Includes bibliographical references and index.
  | Audience: Ages 7-12 | Audience: Grades 3-7 | Summary: "Amazing
  photography accompanies engaging information about the fighting
  abilities of giant otters and caimans. The combination of high-interest
  subject matter and light text is intended for students in grades 3
  through 7"– Provided by publisher.
Identifiers: LCCN 2021039716 (print) | LCCN 2021039717 (ebook) | ISBN
  9781644876244 (library binding) | ISBN 9781648346873 (paperback) | ISBN
  9781648346354 (ebook)
Subjects: LCSH: Otters–Juvenile literature. | Caimans–Juvenile literature.
Classification: LCC QL737.C25 D68 2022 (print) | LCC QL737.C25 (ebook) |
  DDC 599.769–dc23
LC record available at https://lccn.loc.gov/2021039716
LC ebook record available at https://lccn.loc.gov/2021039717

Editor: Rebecca Sabelko   Designer: Josh Brink

Printed in the United States of America, North Mankato, MN.

TABLE OF CONTENTS

THE COMPETITORS 4

SECRET WEAPONS 10

ATTACK MOVES 16

READY, FIGHT! 20

GLOSSARY 22

TO LEARN MORE 23

INDEX 24

THE COMPETITORS

Dangerous **predators** make their homes in and around the Amazon River. Giant otters are some of the largest. These speedy swimmers can chase down almost any **prey**.

Caimans often compete with giant otters for food. They sneak through the water, looking for their next meal. Who would win in a clash between these two predators?

Giant otters are the largest otters in the world. These **mammals** grow to be around 6 feet (1.8 meters) long. Their bodies are covered in dark brown fur.

Giant otters make their homes in the rivers and lakes of the Amazon **Basin**. They live in groups of up to 20 otters. They are most active during the day.

RIVER WOLVES

In South America, giant otters are also known as river wolves.

GIANT OTTER PROFILE

LENGTH
AROUND 6 FEET
(1.8 METERS)

WEIGHT
UP TO 75 POUNDS
(34 KILOGRAMS)

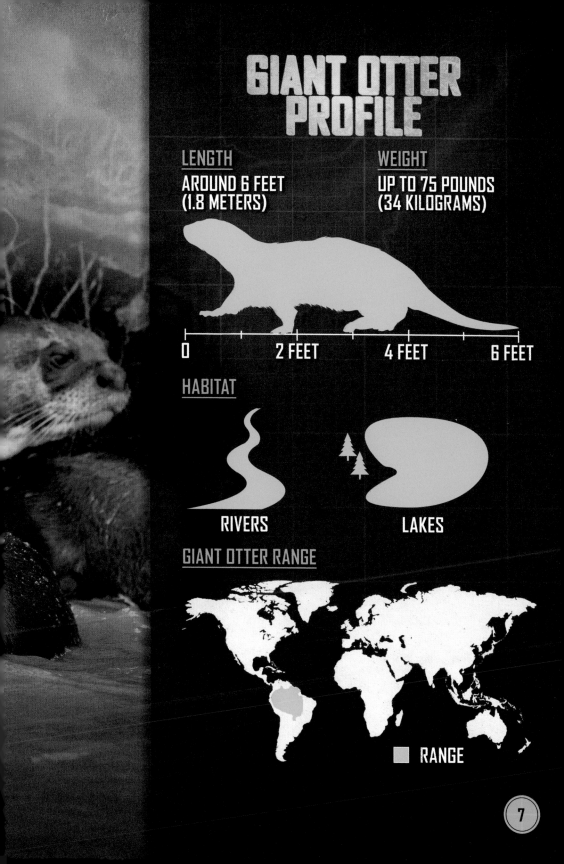

0   2 FEET   4 FEET   6 FEET

HABITAT

RIVERS   LAKES

GIANT OTTER RANGE

RANGE

BLACK CAIMAN PROFILE

LENGTH
MORE THAN 19 FEET
(5.8 METERS)

WEIGHT
AROUND 1,000 POUNDS
(454 KILOGRAMS)

0   5 FEET   10 FEET   15 FEET   20 FEET

HABITAT

RIVERS   LAKES   WETLANDS

BLACK CAIMAN RANGE

■ RANGE

Caimans are **reptiles**. They make their homes near rivers and lakes in Central and South America. Their heads are wide and flat. They have round noses.

There are six different **species** of caiman. The black caiman is the largest species. Black caimans can reach more than 19 feet (5.8 meters) long!

BLACK CAIMAN

SECRET WEAPONS

Giant otters are built to hunt in water. They have long tails that grow to lengths of more than 27 inches (68.6 centimeters). Their tails help them swim over 9 miles (14.5 kilometers) per hour as they chase prey!

20	20	20
OVER 9 MILES (14.5 KILOMETERS) PER HOUR	UP TO 30 MILES (48 KILOMETERS) PER HOUR	UP TO 6 MILES (9.7 KILOMETERS) PER HOUR
GIANT OTTER	YACARE CAIMAN	HUMAN

Caimans have strong tails that push them through water. They do not have to use their feet when they swim!

SECRET WEAPONS

LONG TAIL

WHISKERS

SHARP TEETH

WHISKERS

Giant otters use their sense of sight to hunt. But their whiskers help them find prey in **murky** water. They feel the movements of fish.

CAIMAN

 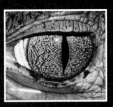 

STRONG TAIL   TRANSPARENT   POWERFUL JAWS
                EYELIDS

Caimans often wait for prey underwater. They have eyes and **nostrils** on top of their heads. This lets them peek out of the water. **Transparent** eyelids help them see underwater.

Giant otters have sharp teeth. Their teeth allow them to tear into their prey. They rip off chunks of meat.

Caimans have powerful jaws lined with cone-shaped teeth. They snap their jaws around prey. Their sharp teeth sink into **flesh** and hold on tight.

ATTACK MOVES

A GOOD MEAL

Giant otters need a lot of food. They may eat up to 9 pounds (4 kilograms) of food in one day!

Giant otters hold onto their food with their front paws. But sometimes their prey bites back. The otters bite their prey's heads off first to avoid getting bitten.

Caimans **ambush** their prey. They are nearly **invisible** underwater as they sneak up on animals. When they get close enough, caimans spring toward their meal!

Giant otters mostly hunt on their own.
But when prey is large or dangerous,
giant otters hunt in groups. They work
together to take down their prey.

Once caimans make a catch, they crush the animal with their strong jaws and teeth. If bites do not finish the prey, caimans drag it underwater.

MORE TEETH

Caimans often lose their teeth. Worn teeth fall out. New teeth grow in their place!

READY, FIGHT!

A caiman waits silently for a meal. It spots a giant otter on the riverbank. It sneaks in close and attacks! But the otter escapes the caiman's snapping jaws.

Luckily for the otter, its family is nearby. The otters team up to bite the caiman over and over again. Before long, the caiman is defeated!

GLOSSARY

ambush—to carry out a surprise attack

basin—the area drained by a river

flesh—the soft parts of an animal

invisible—impossible to see

mammals—warm-blooded animals that have backbones and feed their young milk

murky—muddy and unclear

nostrils—the two openings of the nose

predators—animals that hunt other animals for food

prey—animals that are hunted by other animals for food

reptiles—cold-blooded animals that have backbones and lay eggs

species—kinds of animals

transparent—able to be seen through

TO LEARN MORE

AT THE LIBRARY

Downs, Kieran. *Nile Crocodile vs. Hippopotamus*. Minneapolis, Minn.: Bellwether Media, 2022.

Rector, Rebecca Kraft. *The Amazon Rainforest*. Lake Elmo, Minn.: Focus Readers, 2018.

Schuh, Mari. *Animals of the Amazon Rain Forest*. North Mankato, Minn.: Capstone Press, 2022.

ON THE WEB

FACTSURFER

Factsurfer.com gives you a safe, fun way to find more information.

1. Go to www.factsurfer.com

2. Enter "giant otter vs. caiman" into the search box and click 🔍.

3. Select your book cover to see a list of related content.

INDEX

Amazon Basin, 6
Amazon River, 4
ambush, 17
attacks, 21
bite, 16, 19, 21
Central America, 9
color, 6
eyes, 13
food, 5, 16, 17, 21
fur, 6
groups, 6, 18
habitat, 4, 6, 7, 8, 9
hunt, 10, 12, 18
jaws, 15, 19, 21
mammals, 6
name, 6
noses, 9
nostrils, 13
predators, 4, 5

prey, 4, 10, 12, 13, 14, 15,
    16, 17, 18, 19
range, 7, 8
reptiles, 9
sight, 12
size, 4, 6, 7, 8, 9, 10
South America, 6, 9
species, 9
speed, 4, 10, 11
swim, 4, 10, 11
tails, 10, 11
teeth, 14, 15, 19
water, 5, 10, 11, 12, 13,
    17, 19
weapons, 12, 13
whiskers, 12

The images in this book are reproduced through the courtesy of: Johnny Giese, front cover (giant otter);
Mats Brynolf, front cover (caiman); PhotocechCZ, pp. 2-3, 14, 20-24; nwdph, pp. 2-3 (giant otter right),
12 (sharp teeth), 20, 22, 24 (giant otter right); Chris Bruskill / FLPA, pp. 2-3, pp. 20-24 (caiman); Walter
Mario Stein, p. 4; Uwe Bergwitz, p. 5; GTW, pp. 6-7; Toniflap, pp. 8-9; Luciano Candisani, pp. 10, 17;
Nature Picture Library/ Alamy, p. 11; Giedriius, pp. 12, 15, 19 (giant otter left); OSTILL is Frank
Camhi, p. 12 (long tail); Vladimir Wrangel, p. 12 (whiskers); Annalucia, p. 13; Smiler99, p. 13
(strong tail); iliuta goean, p. 13 (transparent eyelids); Sébastien Lecocq/ Alamy, p. 13 (powerful jaws);
Reto Buhler, p. 16; blickwinkel/ Alamy, p. 18; FLPA/ Alamy, p. 19.